Near or Far

Where's Eddie?

Daniel Nunn

Illustrations by Steve Walker

Raintree

Hide and Seek

www.raintreepublishers.co.uk
Visit our website to find out
more information about
Raintree books.

To order:
☎ Phone 0845 6044371
🖹 Fax +44 (0) 1865 312263
🖳 Email myorders@raintreepublishers.co.uk

Customers from outside the UK please telephone +44 1865 312262

Raintree is an imprint of Capstone Global Library Limited,
a company incorporated in England and Wales having its
registered office at 7 Pilgrim Street, London, EC4V 6LB –
Registered company number: 6695582

Edited by Dan Nunn, Rebecca Rissman, and Sian Smith
Designed by Joanna Hinton-Malivoire
Picture research by Mica Brancic
Originated by Capstone Global Library Ltd.
Production by Victoria Fitzgerald
Printed and bound in China by Leo Paper Products Ltd

ISBN 978 1 406 23896 9 (hardback)
16 15 14 13 12
10 9 8 7 6 5 4 3 2 1

ISBN 978 1 406 23902 7 (paperback)
17 16 15 14 13
10 9 8 7 6 5 4 3 2 1

British Library Cataloguing in Publication Data
Nunn, Daniel.
  Near or far : where's Eddie?. – (Hide and seek)
  1. English language–Synonyms and antonyms–Pictorial
  works–Juvenile literature.
  I. Title II. Series
  428.1-dc23

Acknowledgements
We would like to thank the following for permission to reproduce
photographs: Shutterstock pp.5 (© Africa Studio), 6 (© smereka),
7 (© lkphotographers), 8 (© Steve Heap), 9 (© paul prescott), 10
(© Ihnatovich Maryia), 11, 12 (© Dhoxax), 13, 14 (© Claire Willis),
15, 16 (© Ljupco Smokovski), 17, 18 (© Tungphoto), 19, 20 (© R
Gombarik), 21 (© Renewer), 22 (© aboikis), 23 (© Kalin Eftimov).

Front cover photograph of a field reproduced with permission
of Shutterstock (© Majeczka). Back cover photograph of train
reproduced with permission of Shutterstock (© Claire Willis).

Every effort has been made to contact copyright holders of any
material reproduced in this book. Any omissions will be rectified in
subsequent printings if notice is given to the publisher.

Contents

Be careful when you hide!
Eddie can hide in places where people can't. Hiding inside things can be very dangerous. Always ask an adult if it is safe first.

Meet Eddie the Elephant

This is Eddie the Elephant.

5

Near

6 Sometimes Eddie hides **near** things.

Far means a long way from something.

Find Eddie!

Can you find Eddie?
Count to 10, then off you go!

Eddie is **far** from the train.

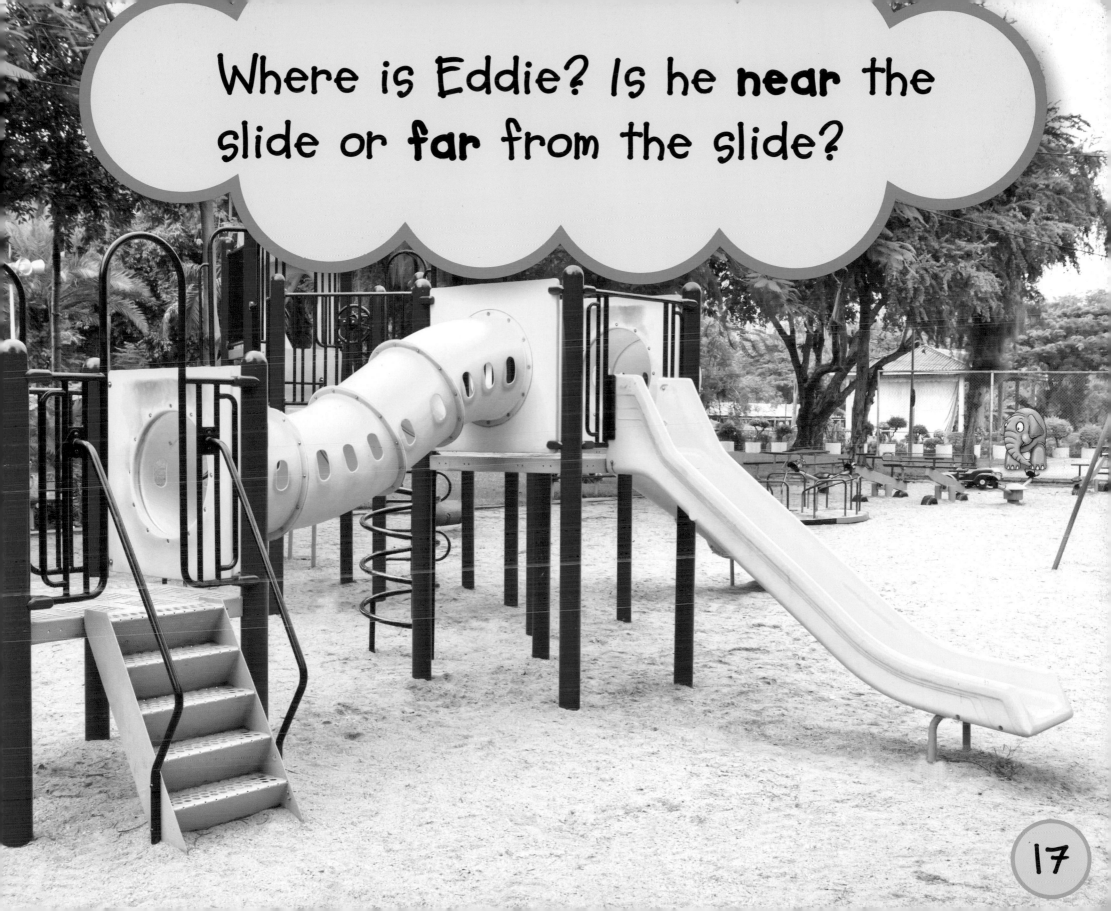

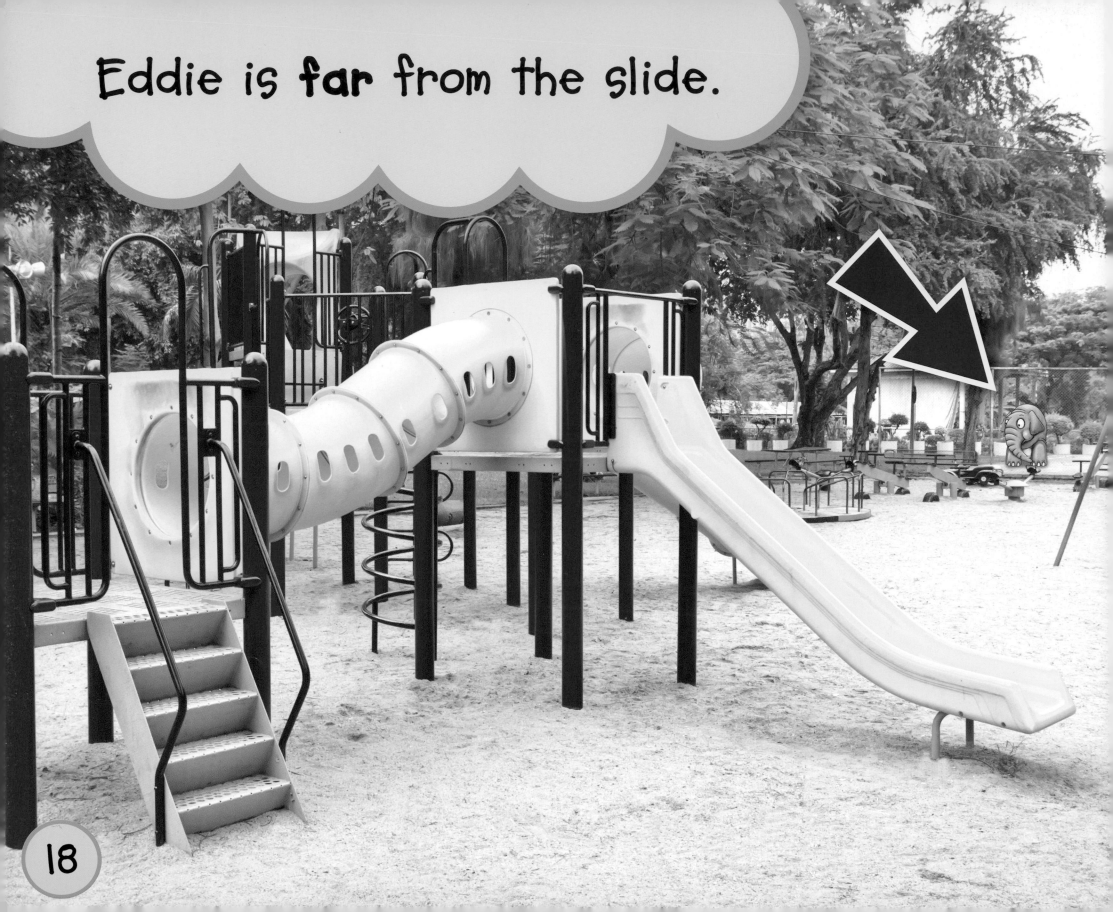

Eddie is **far** from the slide.

18

Where is Eddie? Is he **near** the giraffes or **far** from the giraffes?

19

Eddie is **far** from the giraffes.

True or false?

1. Eddie is **far** from the fountain. True or false?

You can find the answers on page 24.

2. Eddie is **near** the books.
True or false?

Answers and more!

True or false?

1. False! Eddie is **near** the fountain.
2. True! Eddie is **near** the books.
3. False! Eddie is **far** from the bench.

Where can Eddie hide next?

Look around the room you are in.

What could Eddie hide **near**?

What could Eddie hide **far** from?